AGAINST VANISHING

By Cristin O'Keefe Aptowicz

Copyright: Cristin O'Keefe Aptowicz, 2025

All rights reserved. No part of this book may be used, performed, or reproduced in any manner whatsoever without written permission from the publisher except in the case of brief quotations embodied in critical articles or reviews.

First Edition
ISBN: 978-1949342703

Cover Design by David Graham
Interior Layout by Arkadii Pankevich
Edited by Wess Mongo Jolley and Sarah Kay
Proofread by Wess Mongo Jolley
Author Photo by Ernest Cline

Type set in Bergamo

Printed in the USA

Write Bloody Publishing
Los Angeles, CA

Support Independent Presses
writebloody.com

Against Vanishing

ଔ

by Cristin O'Keefe Aptowicz

Write Bloody

America's Independent Press

Los Angeles, CA

www.writebloody.com

TABLE OF CONTENTS

Inheritance 9

Part One: Know Your Purpose 11

    The First Wedding Was Just For Us 12
    The Family Wedding 13
    On Listening. 14
    Can't Hardly Wait. 15
    Process 16
    On Telling Poet Friends
    How to Write More Poetry 17
    Maps. 18

Part Two: Be Present 21

    Trying. 22
    GYN Form, 2016 24
    Release 25
    Signs 26
    Two Lines 27
    Time Line 28
    Early 29
    GYN Form, 2017 (Winter). 30
    Division 31
    Text to My Best Friend, 2/26/17, 2:34pm. 33
    Waiting Room 34
    911 West 38th Street, 2nd Floor, Room 12, 8:18am 36
    Moonlight. 37
    Keynote 39
    Hotel Zaza, Room 308, 4:47am 41
    4:47am 43
    Follow Up 45
    Bed Rest. 46
    Algorithm 47
    Indulgence 48
    GYN Form, 2017 (Spring) 49

Prescription 50
Filled. 52
Test. 53
GYN Form, 2017 (Summer) 54
Text to My Best Friend, 8/1/17, 3:25pm. 55
Natural Disasters. 57
On the Definition of the Word Complete 60
Blood Type. 61
GYN Form, 2017 (Fall) 62
Schrodinger's Motherhood 63
The Bad News Outfit 64
After So Much Loss, I was Afraid I'd No Longer
    Enjoy Making Love 66
On the Eve of the First Due Date 67
National *Your Dog Hates Your Guts* Day. 68
Text to My Best Friend, 12/1/17, 1:44pm. 70
GYN Form, 2017 (Late Winter) 72
Text to My Best Friend, 12/19/17, 4:53pm. 73
Nine Weeks 74
Seventeen Weeks 75
My Adidas 76
Twenty-Seven Weeks 78
On Finally Unpacking Gifts from the Baby Shower 79
The Last Bad Mother's Day 80
Radio Radio. 83

Part Three: Act Decisively 85

Honking Through Red Lights 86
Body Parts 87
39 Weeks 88
Dr. Feel Good 89
Show Time. 90
Day One. 91
Day Two. 92
Day Three. 93
Day Four. 95
Day Five 96

 Day Six 97
 One Week 98

Part Four: Don't Get Attached to the Results 101
 To My Friend Who Is Getting
  A Follow-Up Sonogram 102
 GYN Form, 2018 (Fall) 103
 If You Had Been a Boy 104
 Hand Me Downs 105
 If You *Are* a Boy 106
 Ashland, OH 107
 One Year 108
 Before We Really Knew 109
 Text from My Physician Brother-in-Law about
  Why It is Critical to Self-Isolate, 3/13/20. 110
 At the Beginning of a Possible Pandemic,
  I Dream of the Room My Mother Died In 111
 Turning Three During a Pandemic 113
 After My Vaccination 114
 Love in the Time of COVID 115
 On the Occasion of My Husband Going On his First
  Business Trip in Two Years, and Then Deciding the
  Very Next Day That He was Coming Home Early 116
 Tambourine! Tambourine! Tambourine! 117
 Oh, New York 119
 My Little New York 121
 Parallel 122
 On the Six-Year Anniversary of My Mother's Passing 123
 My Dead Ancestors Try to Explain To Me
  How I'm Missing the Point 124
 On Lowering Standards 125
 She Reaches Out, Says, *I Love You* 126
 Ownership 128
 Present 129

Acknowledgements 130
About the Author 134

Inheritance

When my mother passed, my father gave me her journals,
years of them. In one, she collected only the words
of other writers and I spent days reading the wisdom
of other people through the lens of what was important
about them to my mother. Pages of it. Pages and pages,
except one page, for which there were no citations.
My mother figuring something out for herself, four ideas:
>*Know Your Purpose.*
>*Be Present.*
>*Act Decisively.*
>*Don't Get Attached to the Results*

She marked this as "<u>TRUE WORK</u>."
All CAPS.
Underlined.
And I made it the wallpaper for my phone.
I made it my daily mantra. I made it my sacred goal:
>*Know Your Purpose. Be Present. Act Decisively.*
>*Know Your Purpose. Be Present. Act Decisively.*
>*Know Your Purpose. Be Present. Act Decisively.*

My mother reminding me every day:
>*Know Your Purpose. Be Present. Act Decisively.*
>*Know Your Purpose. Be Present. Act Decisively.*
>*Know Your Purpose. Be Present. Act Decisively.*

And when I found myself bruised, hurt, those times
when I wasn't sure I recognized myself, when I stood
uncertain if I trusted where my road was taking me,
I turned to it, turned to her, her handwriting
the closest I could get to hearing her voice again,
seeing her easy smile again, closest I could get
to reaching across time and space to whisper to me,
with a wink:
>*And baby, remember, don't get attached to the results.*

PART ONE:

KNOW YOUR PURPOSE

The First Wedding Was Just For Us

Let me start here, holding your hands
in the office of the judge we just met.
He tells us to look at each other,
but I can't at first: my body
like champagne, full of stars,
my hands shaking on the other side
of your steady ones, my cheeks
hot and throbbing from smiling. Oh love,
this secret moment, just us two,
you in your blue shirt & grey jeans,
me in my simple blue dress with pockets,
the judge in his robe, the day wrapped
in its light, the clouds, white and gold,
strung in the window like bunting.
It is here, husband, on that worn carpet,
that we both say the words that do it,
make our two into one, tears streaming
down my face. When I push the ring
onto your finger, I kiss it, quickly,
before the judge can say anything else.

The Family Wedding

I wake up at four-thirty the morning
of our wedding as the sun blooms
on the Delaware River outside the hotel.

My best friend sleeps in the bed,
five & a half months pregnant.
I stand taking pictures of the sun

rising, inch by inch. In the shower,
my father's words from last night's
rehearsal dinner rattle in my head,

how he told everyone that my getting
married *was no guarantee*. The absence
of my mother rings my heart's bell.

How she would have hollered, *BRUCE!*
and swatted him open-handed. How
the room would've burst into laughter.

How in the shower I burst into tears,
not of sadness, but not of joy. Rather,
because of the humanness of it all:

the morning of my wedding, my mother
still dead, the sun still shining, life sleeping
and growing in the hotel bed from which

I just woke. In another hotel room
on another floor: my soon-to-be husband,
my soon-to-be stepkid, still sleeping.

I thought of my mom: her laugh, the way
her shoulders rose to meet her ears when
she smiled, when she really smiled,

her eyeroll and grin. *It's gonna be
a great party,* she would've told me,
Enjoy it! So I stepped out and I did.

On Listening

My body has always been the rattle in my car
I learned to live with. I never expected anyone
to love it like I did, but I always knew the value
of my heart: that soft lumpy sofa where the people
I love could fling themselves on, find comfort.
I listen. I read once that people can invent themselves
through the act of another person just listening,
if only they can find a person who will listen,
who will hear them. I listen. I remember.

The first time my now husband ever saw me dressing,
he said, *How did I never notice your body before?*
It's perfect. And I didn't know what to say. I rolled
my eyes, tugging my shirt over my soft everything.
I remember writing in those early days, *more beautiful
women have loved you, more talented*, and that is how
I actually thought a love poem to him should start:
with an acknowledgment that I know he has done
better, could do better, could do better than *me*.

Our love grew from a long friendship, and that felt
like cheating somehow, like I accidentally invented us
through my listening, through being there for him.
To sit with him was to know my purpose: shelter.
Years later, finally alone, we strip off our clothes
I can't believe I get to have sex with you, I tell him.
He laughs, his hands searching over the length of me.
My body feels invented by his hands, by his listening
to me, and through him, my body finally feels perfect,
finally *is* perfect, finally a thing to be loved.

Can't Hardly Wait

If I'm honest, it still feels like I'm getting away
with something I shouldn't. Sex, a teenage mystery
that I was still trying figure out in college… and after.

I'd imagine what it would will be like to unbutton a shirt,
fan fingers across a chest, the buzzing, sparking potential
of it all, a good danger. Was it that focus, that lonesome

study, that stitching of theory and feeling, and (*be honest*)
lack of opportunity that makes our love so spinning
and surreal? How it felt to be young in a speeding car

and no one could stop you, the wind dragging
its fingers through your hair, drowning out
the loud belts of your own joy-drunk laughter,

your own bold shouts into the dark? Each time it ends,
I promise myself I will handle it better next time,
be more in control, enjoy it like a grown-up,

like the actual factual adult that my driver's license
says I am. But as soon as the door to our bedroom
clicks, I feel it again: the radio turned up,

flat road ahead, the streetlamps keeping
a steady rhythm over our laughing, incredulous faces.
Can you believe we are allowed to do this?

To be given the keys to each other's bodies,
to take them out for spin, pedal to floor,
determined to see what this baby can really do.

Process

My first poems were written on paper my mom
pinched from her job at the IRS, and I kept them,
holy as relics, in a Trapper Keeper under my bed.
Later I graduated to thick black journals, tear stains
circled and notated, offered up to future readers
as proof: I *meant* it. Later, I'd write on the subway,
write at the bar, write at work, the Word doc hidden
under the spreadsheets and invoices I was actually
being paid to create. I never worried about being
good. That was never the point. The point was
to insist, to persist, to claim the land simply by
planting a flag, daring someone to tell me it wasn't
art. Years later, I sit at the desk in our laundry room,
remind myself to stay loose, to stay open, to put
every rock that catches my eye into the tumbler,
letting go of the hope that it will become a jewel,
letting go of the fear that it will simply dissolve
into dust.

On Telling Poet Friends How to Write More Poetry

It's so easy,
I tell them,

to write a poem
every day

you just need
to sit down

and check in
with your

self and then
lower your

standards
of what

a poem
is.

Maps

I.

In our earliest months he told me,
*I can feel you wanting me to promise you
things that I can't promise you,*
and I was dumbstruck how wrong he was.

II.

The first time he told me he wanted to marry me
I said, *Are you saying that because it's what you think
I want? Because you told me from the beginning
you didn't think you'd ever get married again,
and I believed you.*

But feelings can change, he said.

Okay, I said, *but they also don't have to.
You don't owe me anything.*

III.

When he finished the book he'd struggled
to finish, and I still found myself in his bed,
I burst into tears.

I don't understand, I wept into his pillow,
my weary brain undone by his kind hands
on my body, *you don't need me anymore.*

Of course, I still need you, he said,
*but you aren't here because I need you.
You are here because I love you.*

I don't understand, I kept repeating,
I don't understand, I don't understand.

IV.

When the judge asked us to hold hands,
I was surprised by how real it all was.
His hands were real. The room was real.
The words were real.

When he said it—*I do*—and kissed me,
I thought the world would explode around me.

Afterwards, he asked the waitress to hold
the avocado, and then said, *Wait. Nevermind.
My wife likes avocado, so I'll give it to her.*

It was the first time I ever heard him
call me his wife, and I burst into tears
again. The waitress smiled and said,
She must really like avocado!

V.

Husband, life with you is nothing I expected,
nothing I prepared myself for, nothing I could
have predicted. What else, I wondered, could I
not foresee? What else should I leave space for?

VI.

When the automated voice of my pharmacy called
to let me know that I needed to contact my doctor
if I intended to refill my birth control prescription,
I listened to the message fully, completely, twice,
before it disconnected. Then I went on with my day.

PART TWO:

BE PRESENT

Trying

My agent tells me I am like her:
filled with testosterone.

That's why we are so aggressive,
she says, *why we don't take shit*

from anyone. But, she explains,
it is the same thing that makes it

harder for a baby to stick.
So, she suggests I stop feeding

that part of me. *I mean that literally*,
she says, giving me a list of foods

I need to start refusing: all breads,
rices, sugar of any kind, including fruit.

I need to exercise more to further
drain myself, swallow vitamins

by the handful, morning and night.
I shrink, which my husband says

doesn't seem right. There is something
I'm told to give up but find I can't: coffee.

I love too much this small cup of rage
that pushes me forward, makes me feel

alive, feel worthy of life, feel like myself
at this time when I mostly feel like

a failed test, like a series of failed tests,
like months and months of failed tests,

like a sack of useless, like a shuttered
museum, like an empty circus tent

whose buzzing spotlight keeps shining
on a relentlessly empty stage.

GYN Form, 2016

<u>Age</u>: 37
<u>Number of Pregnancies</u>: 0
<u>Number of Miscarriages</u>: 0
<u>Number of Live Births</u>: 0

Release

After months of trying, I couldn't anymore.
It was a sign, I felt, of what wasn't going to be.

I told my husband I needed it to be my choice
to stop, and called my doctor's office to restart

my birth control prescription. But they couldn't
do it over the phone. I needed to come in,

see the doctor. *I can't do it*, I told the nurse,
though the truth was I didn't want to do it,

to have that conversation. At my last visit I was
prescribed prenatal vitamins. The nurse paused,

generously said my annual was in three months,
and could I just wait until then? *Yes,* I told her,

and scheduled the appointment. I updated
my husband, told him we were going rogue,

believing that it meant nothing. What difference
was being on birth control when you couldn't

get pregnant if you tried? Or rather when...
And so, that was it. That was it.

Until it wasn't.

Signs

It was early February when I realized
I wasn't sleeping the whole night anymore.

I kept waking and wanting to stretch.
My back was rubbery dough.

I even went to yoga (*me*, going to *yoga*)
to see if that would fix it, and it was awful.

I kept getting dizzy and hot. I struggled.
Days later I peed on an ovulation strip,

hoping that might explain it. Months earlier,
my doctor had said I wasn't ovulating,

and so when the strip came back positive,
I thought, *Well, that's weird,*

but there it is. This is what ovulating
feels like. That explains it.

It wasn't until I was in the dark
of a movie theater that I woke up

to the other possibility. I squeezed
my arms to hug myself as a test,

and my breasts immediately throbbed
in response. That night went to sleep

alone, woke up at 4am again. This time,
I took a test with me to the bathroom.

I set my alarm for three minutes.
I didn't think

it was possible.

Two Lines

When the test came out positive
the first thing I did was google: *What else
could a positive pregnancy test mean?*

I rushed downstairs where my husband slept,
and my radiant stepkid curled next to him.
I watched them sleep. I didn't wake him.

All day I walked in a half-state. Not sure
if I should tell my husband, because what
if something wasn't right? *No,* I decided,

I'll go to the doctor first. My best friend,
eleven hundred miles away, told me I was
insane. That I needed to tell him, precisely

in case something *was* wrong, so I wouldn't
be alone in it. That night, we crawled into bed
together. At the last moment before he finally

fell asleep, I turned to him and said,
*Are you awake? Because there is something
I have to tell you but I'm afraid.*

I burst into tears, sobbing for so long
he thought I had cancer. He kept rubbing
my back telling me whatever it was,

it would be okay. I sucked in hard breaths,
face down into my pillow, on the precipice.
He didn't know. He didn't know.

And then I said it out loud.

Time Line

He sat up in bed as the truth unraveled,
and he told me he was happy. And the next
morning, he was still happy. And that evening,

he worried. He wasn't in great shape,
and that he needed to get healthier
if he was going to be around for the next

eighteen years. He kept saying, *eighteen years*,
and I told him I felt like an idiot: He didn't
ask for this. I made this mess because

I thought I would only be taking birth control
for symbolic reasons, and because I didn't want
to have a conversation with my doctor.

And he told me it was okay. He was just talking
and he was happy. And that I needed to make
a doctor's appointment. And I told him

I just wanted to take a few more tests.
Just give me until Monday, and then Monday
arrived. There were still two lines,

and we made the earliest appointment
we could, which was in one week.
And then we waited.

Early

That week was the brightest of light.
We could barely look at it, but it was warm.
Our conversations tumbled over each other,

like piles of sleeping puppies waking up,
too young to be able to open their eyes.
We could say it, and then we couldn't say it.

We held it all so gently. But despite ourselves,
a form was taking shape. Halloweens and
Fourths of July. The nursery we could put

in the corner of the bedroom. How this thing
we didn't think was possible might be.
In the doctor's office, they put the sonogram

up on the screen. They told me it was
too early for a heartbeat. That I was much
earlier in my pregnancy than thought,

but they printed out the pictures
and gave them to us with a bag that said,
You can't spell Momentous without MOM!

GYN Form, 2017 (Winter)

<u>Age</u>: 38
<u>Number of Pregnancies</u>: 1
<u>Number of Miscarriages</u>: 0
<u>Number of Live Births</u>: 0

DIVISION

Two days later the call came in,
and it was the nurse who told me

bluntly: *the pregnancy is nonviable.*
The morning before I had woken up

with a start, my body feeling different.
Whatever magic had told me to take

those 4am tests was fading and I began
googling about what the blood tests

could tell me. So when she said
those words—*blighted ovum*—I knew

what it meant. After dividing a few times,
my egg just stopped and my idiot body

didn't notice, and just kept carrying on
when there was no baby. This is why

there was no heartbeat. It was just
a busted egg. I was alone in my car.

I told my husband via text, saying
I was going to drive and cry for a while.

The next day the nurse called again
to confirm, and I asked her if I still needed

to come in for my already scheduled
blood test if I miscarried that weekend,

and she said yes, so that they could
determine if all the tissue was out,

and I remember being mad at how stark
her words were, but relieved she wasn't

sugar-coating it. I waited and nothing.
Next blood test was more of the same.

My doctor told me to get a sonogram
to see what was going on. I knew what

this meant too: They'd offer a D&C
as an alternative to miscarrying naturally.

I hated the idea of it. I hated the wait
too. I hated all of it, especially the fact

that I was here because I couldn't be
bothered to talk to my fucking doctor

about some goddamn birth control.
And so I ate sushi and drank coffee

and cried until the appointment
that Wednesday.

Text to My Best Friend, 2/26/17, 2:34pm

I wish I could just erase the last weeks
& live the rest of my life feeling like
I made the choice not to pursue motherhood.

It feels so exceptionally cruel to be surprised
by the possibility & now just walk around
literally carrying failure in my body

until I bleed it out.

Waiting Room

I told my husband that
during the appointment I wanted him

to stay in the waiting room, that sea
of pregnant women. One asked me

how far along I was, and I told her
Oh, I'm not pregnant.

She replied, *Well, what are you doing
here then?* And I told her that the machines

can see all sorts of things related to
reproductive organs. And she smiled,

*Well, you learn a new thing every day.
But is it that you want a baby?*

My husband leaned over, whispering
that I could leave and wait in the bathroom

and he would text me when they called
my name. I whispered back that if I left now,

I would never, ever come back. They called
my name, and I left him behind. I didn't want

the doctor and technician to have split
the sorry news between the two of us.

Just tell it to me, and I'll handle the rest.
I didn't look at the screen as they did

the initial sweeps. As the doctor scanned,
she asked why I was here and I told her.

She said she was ready to show me
what she found, and I sat up. She said,

*I see a pregnancy in the right place
in the uterus. It's earlier than they thought,*

*I'd say six weeks? And here you can see
the heartbeat, that little pulse.*

*That big pulse is you. That little pulse
is the baby, is the baby's heartbeat.*

911 West 38th Street, 2nd Floor, Room 12, 8:18am

A heartbeat.
A heartbeat.
A heartbeat.

Moonlight

I asked if the tech could bring
my husband in. *We didn't think
it would be a happy visit!*

He came in, and I told him,
There's a twist! and she showed him
what she showed me,

and his eyes and mouth widened
as he saw the little heartbeat.
We held hands. The doctor asked

when my next appointment
with my doctor was, and I told her
There is none! We were told

this was a non-viable pregnancy!
And she said, *Well, I'd suggest
you make one.* And we did.

Two days later, our doctor said,
Well, you scared the heck out of me!
And I said, *You scared the heck out of ME!*

And he showed us the blood tests,
and it was true. All signs pointed
to a failed pregnancy. And yet,

here it was, on the big screen.
The doctor turned up the volume
so we could hear the beat

of our child's heart. But he was still
concerned. Drew more blood.
Put me on a strict supplement regimen.

A nurse came out with a bag that said,
You can't spell Momentous without MOM!
and my husband said, *We already have one.*

We floated home. He was a fighter.
I told my husband I thought it was a boy
because he reminded me of him:

won't stop, can't stop. I swallowed
my pills. Waited. Next appointment
was in two weeks.

Keynote

The blood tests came back, and they were
not good. I needed to come back in for more.
Hopefully the supplements would start

doing their magic. I asked the nurse
to send me the results, and they were
hard to read. I had gotten worse.

My levels were unsustainable for six weeks,
and here I was at seven. My friend
who had had three miscarriages told me

the stuff I was on was what they put her on,
and she went on to have two boys. I was
the invited speaker the next day

at a medical school in Houston.
My husband said I should stay home,
but I told him that I wasn't sure if staying

home and worrying would help.
And I would be surrounded by doctors
if anything did go wrong. The same friend

who had three miscarriages and two babies
told me to try and enjoy it. *Whatever happens,
you won't regret enjoying the time you were pregnant,*

no matter how long it lasts. My husband and I
went to Houston, and my talk was a big success.
We went back to the hotel room, and I told him,

*This was my first time doing something
like that while pregnant! I feel like a little badass!*
and we ate desserts from the mini bar

and fell asleep. The previous night
I had woken up twice with nightmares
about miscarrying, and walked into

my bathroom terrified. But it was nothing.
Now I woke up in strange hotel room, 3am.
Stumbled into the hotel bathroom: again, nothing.

I crawled back into bed, relieved.
Under the covers, I grab my husband's hand.
In his sleep, he squeezes back.

Hotel Zaza, Room 308, 4:47am

I wake up again and walk into the bathroom.
Oh no, I say out loud when I see it:

the dark red that soaked through my underpants,
through my pajamas, dripping now

on to the hotel's white bathroom floor.
Before I know what to think, I feel everything

pour out of me. My husband is asleep
on the other side of the wall, and now there is

blood everywhere. I remove my underwear
and pajamas and move them to the sink.

More red drops appear on the floor.
I try to wipe them up, and they smear.

I throw the tissue into the bowl, but carefully,
to stick them to the side. I don't want my husband

to ask if I am sure. I want for him to see it
for himself if he wants. When I can, I crawl

into bed and sob into his chest. He runs
into the bathroom and comes back to hold me.

*Have you ever read about someone bleeding
that much and the baby still being okay?* he asks.

I shake my head. I have a day's worth of lectures,
and as soon as it's morning, my husband calls

to cancel them. He buys new plane tickets
so we can catch the next flight home. I stuff

my underwear and pajamas into a garbage bag
to leave behind. *It's lucky I had this gig I guess,*

I tell him. *So that this all could happen in a room
I never have to see again.*

4:47 AM

When the baby falls out of me,
it isn't a baby. It is a blueberry.

And the doctors will later tell us
that it was likely so damaged,

it wouldn't have survived birth,
which is why my body expels it

in an ugly hotel room in Houston.
When the baby falls out of me,

I think of every other woman
in the world who could have held

that baby in her, made a baby
with you that actually wanted to live,

but you got stuck with me,
who bleeds through her clothing,

and onto the sheets, and onto the floor,
and who can only say, *Oh no…*

Oh no… Oh no… Oh no…
to the life pouring out of her.

And all I can think
is how you are sleeping

in the next room, and I have
to wake you at some point

with the news
that I'm not the person

you thought I was,
who we thought I was,

who I thought I was
going to be:

a mother.

Follow Up

The next day, I am laying down
and another doctor shows me

the sonogram. It is an empty
auditorium. A late era Rothko.

It is a black and white film
of an empty beach after a storm.

The miscarriage is complete,
she tells me. Complete is such

a funny word in a moment
like this. I am to return

in one week to make sure
there's no further complications.

Bed Rest

After four days of cramping
and clots, my body returns

to itself. Three days later,
my doctor roots around

again, for the last time,
and declares everything

is okay, as good as can be expected.
I don't need to come back.

We return home. It is
what it has always been.

I crawl into bed, and stare
at the corner of the room.

This is what living life is,
my therapist tells me.

*Risks mean hurt sometimes,
but other times they are worth it.*

I reach out to touch my stomach
out of habit, but stop, my hand

hovering above my dumb flesh.
Life, I think. *Life*.

Algorithm

How many times
do I need to google
the word *miscarriage*
in order for the internet
to stop trying to sell me
diapers?

Indulgence

Sushi. Iced coffee by the clear plastic cupful.
Diet soda, filled with demon caffeine. Earl Grey tea
so strong you have to drown it in milk & sugar.
Smoked salmon, piled high on doughy bagels,
or chopped with onion in bright yellow omelets.
Oysters. Blue cheese, and its marbled stinking veins.
Gooey brie barely contained by its rind. Morning eggs
leaking runny yolk all over on my crisp hashbrowns
like sunshine, liquid gold. All of it and more, I happily
said, *goodbye*, gave up, abandoned without reservation,
without pause, without doubt, the morning I found out.
Let it sit untouched on my plate, as I rubbed my belly
like a genie's lamp. As he sat in the roiling waters
himself, I remember telling my husband how good
a hot tub would feel on the aching muscles of my newly
pregnant body. But you can't. Too hot, too bacteria-filled,
too dangerous. When I miscarried, I remember thinking
the same thing, how good it would feel on my body
as it cramped and spasmed, how badly I wanted to cleanse
myself with the unbearable heat of it all. But hot tubs are
forbidden then too, your body more vulnerable than ever.
Weeks later, when I can finally lower myself into one,
empty and emptied, he asks, *Doesn't it feel good?*
Didn't you miss it? I don't answer at first, my body
tensing, overwhelmed. Too much, too fast. But soon
I feel my body relax, learning what it needs to learn:
how to let go.

GYN Form, 2017 (Spring)

Age: 38
Number of Pregnancies: 1
Number of Miscarriages: 1
Number of Live Births: 0

Prescription

To decide not to have a baby
again is not like letting go
of a balloon, dream on a string.

It is not like shutting a door
so tightly that not even the light
escapes. It is not like giving up.

It is like giving in, that hum
of *this will never be you* has always
been your most played song.

And it's not like you didn't want it,
didn't try, weren't happy when
it happened, however brief.

But it was not meant for you. It was not
meant for you. It was not meant for you.
It was not—and so when you message

your doctor to ask if she could send in
your prescription for birth control,
it does not feel bad. You look it up,

and your last message to her asked
the same question. It was from January.
Back then, her nurse asked if you could

wait until your annual in March.
You had said yes, not knowing
the next week you'd conceive.

You also didn't know, couldn't
have known, that the day before
that annual you'd miscarry.

The doctor attempting to comfort
you at that appointment by explaining
how common it was, writing you

a prescription for prenatal vitamins.
But now, you've changed your mind
again. Or did you just change it back?

When I saw you last, you explain
in the message, *I'd just had a miscarriage,
and we weren't sure if we wanted*

*to continue trying… But we've decided
to stop… so if you wouldn't mind…*
The nurse calls me the next day

to let me know that at the pharmacy
the prescription is waiting
for me.

Filled

When I bring the prescription home
I don't take it right away. You don't.
You wait until after your period starts
then you take the first birth control pill.

And so I wait. But still don't after
my cycle starts... not after the next either.
The pills sitting unused in their plastic
bubbles, like talismans, like magic tokens

in a story whose lesson is
Be Careful What You Wish For.
And so I wait, not starting, unsure
if I am keeping myself in limbo,

or in purgatory.

Test

*I keep thinking we will be able to count our time apart
in miscarriages*, I want to text my best friend, *as in
'I haven't seen you in two miscarriages!'* But I don't.
Because it hasn't happened. It hasn't happened *yet*.
The first time it was the blood tests that refused to tell
a lie, even as my body put on its grand, hopeless show,
the doctor turning up the machine so we could hear
the heartbeat: *whoosh-whoosh-whoosh*. But the blood tests?
She kept sucking her teeth at us, showed us the numbers,
the relentless downward spiral of it. *Don't blame me
if you get your heart broke,* she shouted at us, as we chose
to ignore her. Our hearts got broke. And now my body is
a bad magician again, trying to pull a rabbit out of a hat.
It's holding that rabbit in, through every cramp and spasm.
My husband says that until a miscarriage happens, there is
always hope. He says he'll carry that hope for both of us
if he needs to. At the ultrasound, we hold our breath.
The technician searching and searching and searching,
but finding nothing. The blood test cackles in the doctor's
hands. *It says you should be a little over six weeks, but
maybe you are earlier than that… much, much earlier.*
She asks permission to search from the inside. I give it to her.
My husband stares at the screen, that sea of space
with no stars, no ships. The projected due date glows
in green: March 29th. *That's my birthday, you know?*
my husband does not say, although he could have.
*We suggest more blood tests and to come back here
in a week*, the doctor finally says. My husband says
to stay optimistic. *They found nothing*, I tell him.
Well, that also means that they didn't find anything bad,
he says. What can he say? What can anyone say?
Oh, thing that will not appear, thing I have tried to tell
my body to love, to keep, to keep safe, oh heart, oh being,
oh baby. Please stay.

GYN Form, 2017 (Summer)

Age: 38
Number of Pregnancies: 2
Number of Miscarriages: 1
Number of Live Births: 0

Text to My Best Friend, 8/1/17, 3:25pm

The test results show bad news.

My progesterone levels—already so low
that they would normally have indicated
that I haven't ovulated at all—went down
even further.

I'm on an aggressive progesterone
supplement now & they want me back
in on Friday for more blood tests
& a sonogram at the same perinatal
place I went to last time—if I make it
that long—on Monday.

The very sweet nurse is walking over
to the perinatal place herself to see
if she can charm an appointment
that early.

As it stands right now, the appointment
is the day that family arrives, so all in all,
it's a real shit show.

It's like if it's going to end, end now—
not a week from now after I've seen
a sonogram & have a houseful of kids
& babies

I'm sorry. It's a miserable day.
I mean, after the last time, I doubt
they would tell me that the pregnancy
was non-viable again.

They say keep positive thoughts,
but they also post the tests
which just show awful numbers.

Natural Disasters

Two nights before the hurricane hit,
my toilet paper started coming up pink.
Normal, natural is what every friend
and book and website said.

The morning before the hurricane hit,
the toilet paper started coming up bright red,
and I sat at my desk staring at the clock
until 8am, when my OBGYN's office opened.

By then, the first spot appeared. I had stretched
my stupid body and felt it start. The nurse said
they could squeeze me in if I made it there quick.
As I ran upstairs, I could feel it: the undoing.

My poor husband, on the other side of the door,
saying, *We don't know anything yet! It could still
be okay! We just need to get dressed and go!*
We went, and I knew I knew I knew.

That night, it began raining, and didn't let up
for three days. Our inland city got just the edges
of the hurricane, but our sweet friends kept texting
Are you okay? Are you okay? Are you okay?

I had to remind myself they were talking about
the weather. When the power went out, I heard
my husband explain to my sweet and sensitive
stepkid how lucky we were, how there were

people closer to the disaster who had it much worse.
It was true. We were safe and dry and had each other.
But part of me was still there: in the doctor's office,
the day before. The nurse putting towels on the floor,

the doctor asking permission to *collect whatever she could*, how she kept whispering for bigger and bigger specimen cups. That unmagic wand searching inside of me for anything, anything.

How it came back empty-handed, covered in blood. I couldn't look at my husband, or the screen, or the blood. I shut my eyes, stayed in the dark, powerless.

Afterwards, the doctor told me these things, these things just happen. Asked me to remember the sun will come up again tomorrow. But if it did, we didn't see it. All we saw was rain.

When the Attending Nurse During Our Second Miscarriage Confesses That She Has Never Been Pregnant, But If She Was, What I am Going Through Would Be Her Worst Nightmare

Cool.

On the Definition of the Word Complete

The doctor says I have to take one more blood test
to make sure my levels are back to zero, and confirm
the miscarriage is complete. The line outside the lab
is filled with pregnant women. Of course, it is.

Earlier, in the waiting room, I noticed a man and woman
wiping away tears until the man finally excused himself.
When they finally got called in, I whispered to my husband,
Looks like someone else is having a bad day too.

Alone outside the lab, I see the couple again, this time
glowing. Their laughter, uncorked champagne. The woman
is directed to the lab, and seeing her approach, I stand up
to give her my seat. *Oh, no, that's okay*, she demurs.

No, no, I'm not pregnant, I explain, stepping away.
Oh, but I'm barely pregnant, she says, illuminated
with the joy of being able to say it out loud. *Well,
that's pregnant enough,* I say, smiling. She beams

and takes her seat. Through the cinderblock walls,
I hear the quick *whoosh-whoosh-whoosh-whoosh*
of someone else's baby's heartbeat, and hope that,
somehow, it will be my name that will be called next.

Blood Type

The nurse calls to tell me
that the blood work shows
the miscarriage is complete.

*If there were still tissue
inside of you, we'd see something.
But your numbers are zero.*

Everything is gone. Okay,
I tell her. *But I can tell you
your blood type if you want.*

Do you know it? No, I tell her,
and I guess it would be good to know.
Okay then, it's B positive, she says.

Be positive, I reply, *really?*
Yes, she says firmly. I'm not sure
if she gets the irony,

but she repeats it slowly
one more time for me:
Be positive.

GYN Form, 2017 (Fall)

Age: 38
Number of Pregnancies: 2
Number of Miscarriages: 2
Number of Live Births: 0

Schrodinger's Motherhood

The doctor tells me
that all the evidence shows
that overwhelmingly my next
pregnancy should be successful.

Miscarriages are so much more
common than people realize.
Insurance companies don't even
pay for additional tests until
you've had three in a row.

But I've had two in a row, I tell him.

Yes, but again, if you look
at the statistics, two miscarriages in a row
is still an overwhelmingly positive sign
you will have a successful pregnancy!
It's actually stronger indicator of success
than if you were unable to get pregnant
at all!

But three miscarriages in a row, I repeat to him,
and that will show there might be a real problem?

Yes, but you haven't had a third miscarriage.
You've just had the two.

The Bad News Outfit

is what I call it when I pull
my purple tunic over black tights,
paired with a small gray cardigan.

I wear it to the doctor now
when I am pretty sure we are
going to receive bad news.

News about the baby growing,
or rather not growing, inside me.
The look is somber, sober,

but not without color.
I want to assure the doctor
that I know what is coming,

and that I will be okay.
I will not fall apart in his office,
or pepper his useless face

with blame. I will not wail,
or make a scene, or disrupt
the serene, luminous mornings

of the other pregnant women,
sitting in the waiting room—
the *real* pregnant women,

who will actually give birth
to the babies currently thriving,
contentedly, in the wide, happy bellies.

Purple, the color
of my favorite spring crocuses.
Gray, the empty static

of the sonogram screen.
Black, like the ink
in my doctor's pen

as he writes the prescription,
tells me *I'm sorry,*
and sends me home.

After So Much Loss, I was Afraid I'd No Longer Enjoy Making Love

that the act of it would feel
too much like reenacting
a crime. How would it feel
to take him in again knowing
how I keep ruining the things
we love? But my body has
always been a joyful thing
and he such a tireless, eager
celebrater of it.

On the Eve of the First Due Date

My friend who shared my (first) due date gave birth last week.
A boy. *Lucas Edward*. She was the last of the women

who shared the news of their pregnancies shortly after
I miscarried the first time. They didn't know, of course.

I never told them. I didn't want them to feel awkward
about their light, their beam, their expanding globe bodies.

All the babies that were going to be born have been born.
And all the babies that weren't, weren't.

I can't help but think how the second pregnancy,
the second miscarriage, has helped lighten my burden.

I'm relieved this date isn't more devastating for me!
I tell myself again and again until I begin to wonder

what I'm saying. I look at pictures of my friend's baby
and she texts that she can't wait for me to meet him.

I stay home, and hit refresh as I track the package
I sent her as it makes its way across the country.

It's an enormous basket of comfort food.
I keep thinking if it were me, I'd be so hungry.

National *Your Dog Hates Your Guts* Day

is what I've called Halloween ever since adopting two miniature dachshunds and stuffing them into a variety of ridiculous outfits to the delight of friends and family, and certainly not to the delight of those two little rescues, who fume and grouse and refuse to make eye contact. In almost every picture of them dressed in their obscenely tiny costumes—whether shark or superhero or elegant piece of fruit—they are in a simmering state of absolute loathing. In the best photos, though, the ones where I'm holding a bit of waffle just off camera, or maybe a fatty piece of brisket, their ears are perked, their eyes glisten, and it looks as if maybe those two ridiculous beasts might actually enjoy being dressed as Batman and Superman, or Ghostbusters (complete with tiny proton packs), or, of course, being dachshunds, matching hot dogs in buns: one mustard, one ketchup. This year I surprised myself when I realized I was eyeballing yet another costume—*Varsity jackets!* I yelped, *Archie and Jughead!*—when I knew I already had three other costumes lined up for them at home. *What is it about the dog costumes this year?* I wondered, laughing, as I held the tiny jackets up for size, seeing if I could tell just by looking at it if their stubby legs were long enough for the sleeves. *It's because you don't have a baby*, my mind answered unselfconsciously, without a hiccup. And there it was. Dumb in its brutal simplicity.

A few days earlier, at a Halloween event at the zoo, I saw a pregnant woman wearing a skeleton shirt with a fetal skeleton smiling in the curve of the shirt's glow-in-the-dark pelvis bone. How she rubbed her round stomach. How when I looked at her face, I expected her to look beatific. How she honestly just looked exhausted. How I had once imagined wearing a shirt like that if the second pregnancy had just stuck. How if the first one had stuck, the costume I would be buying would not be found next to the pig ears and beef knuckles in the pet section of the grocery store. My God, how I can ruin things. How happy I had just been, picturing my dogs in those jackets. How stupid I feel now, mute in the grocery store aisle, remembering how just yesterday, I ran to my husband, carrying our dogs in my arms dressed in little tuxedos, and held them out for him to admire. *Look at how cute they are*, I screamed, tears streaming from my eyes from laughing, *they look like little humans!*

Text to My Best Friend, 12/1/17, 1:44pm

So it's been a week since I took
my last dose of promenium (*200 mg
of progesterone, daily for a week
to restart cycle*), and I still haven't
gotten my period.

I wrote my doctor today to ask
how long it typically takes.
I had thought it would start as soon
as I stopped taking the pills.

Unfortunately, the doctor's office
closes at noon today, so I missed the window
to get a response.

I'm on day 62 of my cycle,
and haven't done a pregnancy test
since the blood test came back
negative 2 weeks ago.

But I said *Fuck it!*

And even though I was supposed
to use morning urine, I decided
to just do one today and:

[photo: a faintly positive pregnancy test]

Now it's a faint, faint line.

But I just remembered you telling me
that the test doesn't show up for anything other
than pregnancy, so I'm confused.

Should I get like a real deal test?
These are just the tests that come
for free with the ovulation kits.

2017 is the weirdest goddamn year of my
life.

GYN Form, 2017 (Late Winter)

<u>Age</u>: 39
<u>Number of Pregnancies</u>: 3
<u>Number of Miscarriages</u>: 2
<u>Number of Live Births</u>: 0

Text to My Best Friend, 12/19/17, 4:53pm

I was feeling pretty nauseous
and so I opened up a package of saltines,
and the SMELL of *saltines* made me puke!

So needless to say
I am super impressed with this pregnancy!
It is NOT fooling around!

(also when I found out I was pregnant
I was super worried that I might miscarry
on my mom's birthday because I didn't think
I could've handled it...

but today is my mom's birthday and I made it
so I'll take a puke!)

Nine Weeks

When I first got pregnant it was such a surprise, I thought
it must have been a miracle. I asked my mom to help me.

When we were told the baby wasn't viable, but then
we heard the heartbeat, I was sure it was my mom's doing.

When we lost the baby, I didn't know where to turn.
The second pregnancy, I spoke to the baby instead,

told the baby how much I loved it and wanted it to stay.
When they said it wasn't looking good, I told the baby

I understood, but still begged it to stay, to keep trying.
I played the baby music, and stroked it through my belly

and I lost it anyway. When I got pregnant the third time,
I didn't know what to do. I held space for it with nothing,

thought around its edges, didn't ask it to stay because
I couldn't imagine it staying. I held my baby like a breath.

When it was big enough to see on an ultrasound,
the nurse said, *It's putting on a show for you!*

And we watched as the impossible thing wiggled
its little arms and its little legs, fading in and out

of the stage of my womb. I still could not speak its name,
could not call it *baby*, but my husband and I would do

its dance when we spoke of it. Its name was not a name,
it was an action: a defiant sign of life.

Seventeen Weeks

is when the doctors
say your risk of miscarriage
drops to 1%.

I haven't written
a single word about
(you).

*We've beaten the odds
before*, I tell my husband.
You have to have faith,

he replies. It is 17 weeks
and one day, (you)
still seem like a dream,

something that could
vanish the moment
I open my eyes.

17 weeks and
one day, and
I'm still afraid

to say I love (you),
that the possibility
of (you) might be

real. 17 weeks and
one day, and I am
so undone by the idea

of (you) that I am
afraid to even finish
this poem.

My Adidas

Because of his love of Run-DMC,
and because they stopped making
his favorite vintage brand of Nikes,
my husband began wearing Adidas,
the iconic one, you know the one,
all white with three black stripes.
Later, he surprised me with my own,
and I loved to see them together,
husband and wife shoes, unlaced
on our wooden floor. My stepkid's
feet grew so fast one summer,
we swore they would be in adult shoes
in no time. To prove it, my husband
brought them a pair at the smallest
adult size he could find. When they
finally fit months later, we all tooled
around in our Adidas, played
the Run-DMC song, and *danced*.
When my therapist told me it was time
for me to purchase something for the baby,
I flinched. I opened my eyes to her
looking at me, waving her kind hand,
as if to say I was proving her point.
It felt like I could jinx by saying it,
by thinking it: *baby*. (Even now, it is
still hard to type). We had watched
the video of its small limbs dancing
in my stomach, weathered the tests
to see everything come up: *normal*.
But nothing it seems could make me
believe that this small life was possible.
So my therapist said it was time to buy
something for the baby. Just one thing.
Anything. And in an instant, I knew.

Scouted it online, and spent fifty bucks
for the sheer absurdity of it.
The next week, they arrived:
small and perfect, tiny white Adidas,
with black stripes, like her sibling's,
like her father's, like her mother's,
but all hers.

Twenty-Seven Weeks

To imagine you born
is to imagine you disappearing
from my arms,

like being suddenly
awoken from a dream
just as you are about to

whatever. Whatever it is
wasn't real anyway, and you
can't be crushed by what

was never real
and this is how I think
of you, despite your

wriggling under my skin,
and your growing into my ribs
and hips, how the doctor

told me you were resting
high and so close to my lungs
it is no wonder I have

trouble breathing sometimes
and I do, I do, I do. You take
my breath away,

and even in that, that choke
from inside of myself,
I cannot imagine you alive.

On Finally Unpacking Gifts from the Baby Shower

I only do it because
I know I will look crazy

if I don't. Still, I feel crazy
when I do it,

weeping as I snip off tags
and sort into piles.

Will people be mad at me
if the baby is born stillborn?

Who can I entrust to clear
the house of all traces of baby?

And then me, because
if anything happens to her,

you will never see me again.

The Last Bad Mother's Day

This will be the last bad Mother's Day, my husband tells me,
as he helps me leave the bed, and then the house,

and go to an afternoon screening of *The Quiet Place*,
where he is sure no one is bringing their mother, or their baby.

Two years ago, I spent the day in bed, avoiding my phone,
my computer, the TV, my mother's death not quite a year old.

We had spent her last Mother's Day together, and the night
I left to fly back to Texas, she checked into a hospital

and never checked out. In the shadow of her leaving,
I got engaged and married. Then came a year of infertility,

then a pregnancy, and then a miscarriage,
so that next Mother's Day found me back in bed,

avoiding everything again, but doubled.
Empty on both sides. No mother, no child.

This year, *The Last Bad Mother's Day*, finds me
still motherless, with two miscarriages now

to plug into cold doctor's forms,
and a round, full, pregnant belly. Six months

terrifyingly pregnant, and all day, every day,
I am sure I will lose her. My doctors have told me

the constant morning sickness is good,
that gestational diabetes is common

for women my age, that my rapid weight loss
is understandable, all things considered,

but as long as the baby is gaining weight
it is okay. I keep telling my friends,

if I wasn't pregnant, folks would be like, *Girl,
you have cancer! You need to find a new doctor!*

But instead, I do nothing but worry, and cry,
and puke sugar-free lemonade, and, on this day,

sit in the parking lot of a grocery store, waiting
for my husband who said he needed to buy

some essentials since we were out of the house
already. When he arrives with a fat bouquet

of flowers, and a shiny round balloon, no, no,
I tell him, tearful, terrified, I'm not a mother yet.

This is bad luck. *You are already a mother*,
he tells me, *this kid is coming.* I hold the bouquet

on my lap and cry. *I decided while shopping,*
he tells me, *that this was going to be a good*

Mother's Day, the first of many. And it wasn't,
but it was. And the balloon became a talisman,

floating in the air long after it should have laid
on the ground to die. We kept it in the kitchen

so I could see it persevere, as I choked down
vitamins, and checked my blood sugar,

and ate sugarless food I'd be willing
to puke. And it was still floating when

my water broke, still floating as my husband
raced to grab my things, still floating as he

helped me waddle to the garage, and
as I turned to look at the house one last time.

Happy Mother's Day! it told me, spinning,
Happy Mother's Day!

Radio Radio

Pulling out of the driveway,
I reached for the dashboard's radio
and told my shell-shocked self
that whatever song came on
was a sign for this impossible
thing I was carrying
inside of me.

The radio blared out
"Fight for Your Right to Party"
by The Beastie Boys.

All right then, I told my body,
let's go.

PART THREE:

ACT DECISIVELY

Honking Through Red Lights

Driving to the hospital, the contractions gripping
me in their claws, I yelled, *Play rap! Any rap!*

and your dad, blowing his horn through red lights,
pushed the button on the first song he could find:

"Move Bitch" by Ludacris and I rapped along
loudly as the contractions tried to take me under

Move bitch, get out the way!
Get out the way bitch! Get out the way!

I remember thinking even then, that when I tell
this story later, I should probably skip this part.

Body Parts

The doctor on call knew who I was.
She had read my book, she explained,
which I had given her husband,
another doctor, as a thank you gift.
He had been the on-call cardiologist
who performed an emergency procedure
on my husband's heart last November.
It was on my birthday, and I was already pregnant,
but wouldn't know it for a week, and now,
eight months later, that cardiologist's wife
was standing by my bedside, and it all felt
perfect, like fate, like I was writing a poem
in a very complex form I had only just
learned, and I was already nailing.

39 Weeks

The OBGYN shadowing the main doctor was thirty-nine weeks pregnant—one week further than I was! How strange it must've been: a front row seat to an improv spectacle which would drag her on stage soon enough. I was conscious to put on a good show, let her know it was stressful, but fun, that she could handle it. I made sure to take every suggestion from the audience, never broke character, and always responded, *Yes, and…*

Dr. Feel Good

The anesthesiologist was named John,
but my husband called him Dr. Feel Good.
He swanned into the room with straight teeth
and thick ribbons of silver hair. He was also
the only man—other than my husband—who
crossed the threshold of the birthing room.
The entire team of women doctors and nurses
smiled and winked at him. John put the IV
in my left wrist and got it in one try. Then,
he made his way to my back. The needles
for epidurals need go through your spine.
I'd heard it made some people feel paralyzed,
trapped in their own numb bodies. I was nervous.
But Dr Feel Good poured a thick syrup of reassurance,
wrapped in the weighted blanket of his Texas accent.
After easing the needle into my spine, casual as brushing
the hair from my eyes, he told me he wasn't going to lie,
the next few contractions were still going to hurt,
but that they'd be shorter, and keep getting shorter,
until the feeling went away. But Dr Feel Good did
lie, because *all* the pain went away *immediately*.
It was incredible. It was the first time in months
I didn't have nausea or pain. I could still feel my legs.
They just felt like they were in a warm bath. I asked
my husband, "Is this what drugs feel like? Because
if so, I want to be on drugs all the time!" *Settle down,
Aptowicz!* he told me, *Epidurals aren't the kind of drugs
that make you unaware of what you're saying.*
His job done, Dr Feel Good shot me with finger pistols,
gave me wink, and wished me luck, before exiting the room
to find a new woman for whom he would make
her most fervent wish come true.

Show Time

The drugs were so good I could fall asleep,
and so I did. My husband curled up on a bench
by the window. I woke up in not-pain, my body
groaning with an urgent noiseless *something*.
It would rise and fall as I ate ice chips, watching
the monitor, wondering if this was it, if you were
ready to be. When the doctor arrived, she was
surprised to see me awake. I smiled. Examining me,
she confirmed that you were on your way. It was time.
Your dad was still asleep, glasses folded by his head,
wrapped tight in a thin hospital blanket. I was tempted
to let him sleep. Everything already felt like a dream,
one of those dreams where anything was possible.

Day One

I compared it to a gym class,
to the presidential fitness challenge,
to running after a slowly departing bus,
to running up the stairs to an arriving train,
to running on sand on a salty, hot summer day.

I was bent over like a shrimp,
like an old woman, like an Olympic luger,
like a person trying to catch their breath
from laughing so, so hard.

There was no pain. None.
I remembered my mother telling me
the same thing about her labors,
how the drugs worked so good.
We are the lucky ones, I know.
All our energy reserved on the planet
spinning within us,

on that stuck bowling ball,
that wriggling octopus,
that radiant angel,
that blood-smeared, blue-tinted,
thin-limbed wonder who announced
her arrival, *your* arrival, into the world
with not a cry but a squeak,
a DJ scratch,
a thin-edged sigh-gasp
as they placed you, finally, alive
and in my arms.

I told you, *Welcome!*
I told you, *I love you!*
I told you, *I missed you!*
I told you, *We are so happy you are here.*

Day Two

When they put you in my arms
I can't believe you are mine.
That I can hold you as long
as I want: your long eyelashes,
your seashell ears, the squeaks
you make instead of cries.
And I say your name, *Maureen*,
again and again just to hear it.
I missed hearing it. I missed
hearing it said with joy. *Maureen*.
You are here and you are mine.

Day Three

To complain about a pregnancy you were terrified of losing felt
like tempting fate. Still, morning sickness for all three trimesters
plus gestational diabetes meant no crackers, no ginger ale, no rice,
no toast, meant vomiting Crysal Light, meant vomiting string cheese,
meant vomiting tap water, meant vomiting Tums. Each appointment,
the baby grew while my weight dropped. My doctor told me not
to worry. The baby will always get what it needs, told me how
one mother she knew lost teeth after giving birth because the baby
had sucked the calcium right from her bones. This was intended
to make me feel *better*. All I wanted was for the baby to be okay,
and after that, all I wanted was pie. Cherry pie. French Apple pie.
Lemon pie. Peanut butter pie with chocolate and bananas. Anything pie.
Gestational diabetes resolves as soon as you give birth, or at least
that was how it was explained to me, and that was what I explained
to my brother before I instructed him to send me a large box filled
with Tastykake pies from my hometown of Philadelphia. *What flavors?*
he texted back. *All of them*, I replied. Visiting me in the hospital,
my friend Tonie brought four thick slices of my favorite local pie:
The Elvis from Lucy's Fried Chicken, and I burst into tears
when she took them out of the bag. I went to Maureen in the NICU
every three hours to feed her, then back to my room to pump,
and then I would treat myself to one serving of pie: *a little treat!*
I'd fall asleep so happy. On the third day, the nurse woke me up
to take my blood for testing. *Testing for what?* I asked. *Blood sugar,*
she said, *we want to make sure your gestational diabetes is resolved
before we release you.* I asked if it made any difference that I had
been eating pie. *How much pie are we talking about?* she asked
with a reassuring smile. *One slice of pie every three hours since
the baby was born*, I replied. *Where are you getting all this pie?!*
she said shocked, and hopefully a little impressed. *Family,*
I explained, *friends*. She shrugged, told me we could skip the test.

If it hadn't resolved, I'd probably be having symptoms. She left to complete the rest of the forms by herself and I was left to celebrate with some pie.

Day Four

I knew you were my blood
when you took my breast
into your mouth to eat,
legs tense, toes spread
with absolute pleasure

Day Five

I am checked out of the hospital,
but moved into a room within a suite
of Ronald McDonald House apartments
down the hall from the NICU.

You are in the NICU for monitoring,
just until your glucose levels regulate
and your jaundice resolves, and I am
so happy to be so close to you.

But now the rooms I pass are for parents
whose babies aren't just there for monitoring:
the chapels, the grief counseling rooms,
the library of worn, never-wanted books.

Every three hours I walk past them all,
quietly, reverently, gratefully,
my breasts throbbing, I move towards
your warm and hungry body, waiting for me.

Day Six

How can I sleep
when she is living
& breathing right there,
over there, just over there,
we are home, we are home,
she is home & she is alive

One Week

She wakes me up
ten minutes before
the anniversary
of her birth.

I am too busy
trying to settle
her down to get
the timing exactly
right.

Playing "Diamonds
on the Soles of her Shoes"
on my phone
as she nurses.

Outside, dawn is beginning,
but very distantly—all gray
and quiet.

And I look at the clock,
remember how it was
just a week ago, when
she arrived.

How she did not break me
though I swore she would.

In some way, getting stuck
so they would have to cut her
out of me, or born, but
rushed away from me,
something wrong, something
wrong wrong wong,

or not arrive at all, still and gray,
lost at the end anyway,

But she arrived,
quickly and painlessly, impossibly,
my body widened to make room
for her. How I felt a brushing
against my thighs, how I thought
it felt like a sea creature swimming
into the air.

Her dad holding my head up,
my hands gripping my thighs.

One week later, I listen to her
breathe, as her body falls away
from my breast, my nipple
weeping from our closeness.

How she is here & real & warm
& sighing in her sleep, despite
everything.

One week later & mine.

PART FOUR:

DON'T GET ATTACHED TO THE RESULTS

To My Friend Who Is Getting A Follow-Up Sonogram

Is friend too strong a word? It probably is. You're an artist
I love whom I once nominated for a residency. You wrote me
to let me know you couldn't do it because you were pregnant.
It was unexpected. But you were happy.

When you miscarried you wrote to let me know. I told you
about my miscarriages, and those of my friends. I wasn't
sure of your dark luck, if the women in your life
have crossed their finish lines, unscathed.

My friend Tonie said, *At our age, to be pregnant
and not be scared is to be stupid.* But oh, how I wanted
to be stupid. That brand of blissful stupid. But instead,
I held my breath at every appointment.

During our third pregnancy, my husband held my hand
as we walked into the building which had housed so much
bad news. *One day, we'll have positive associations
with this place, I promise*, he said. And we did. We did.

Oh friend, whom I have never met, but whose grief
I helped hold for a bit, today you are pregnant again.
Today anything is possible. I hope your horizon stays
distant. I hope your love stays stupid. I hope, I hope.

GYN Form, 2018 (Fall)

<u>Age</u>: 40
<u>Number of Pregnancies</u>: 3
<u>Number of Miscarriages</u>: 2
<u>Number of Live Births</u>: 1

If You Had Been a Boy

we had a long list of names under consideration. I told your father I was open to Ernest Cline the Third, which he immediately vetoed as he was already well aware of how hard life is for a kindergartener named after a muppet. But I wonder if he would have considered it. Your father liked Kurt, after Kurt Vonnegut, one of his favorite authors, and Kurt Russell, one of his favorite actors, but a kid named Kurt teased me in the fourth grade, so I don't think I could've let that happen. Next, I pitched hard for Ashland Philadelphia Cline, named after our hometowns, and we could've called you "Ash," but your dad told me he left his hometown as soon as he could and therefore didn't want to name his child after it. It was then that I realized your initials could mimic the initials of DeLorean Motor Company, glittering on the grille of your father's beloved car, we started running through names that start with D and M, but we already knew too many Dans and Davids and Derricks. And then your father remembered a name from a movie your older sibling made us go see which featured a gamer named Digby, and I remembered that one of your father's favorite films has a character mentored by a man named Lord Mandrake, so for the last week when we didn't know what you'd be, we were thinking of calling you *Digby Mandrake Cline,* and it was the clear frontrunner, until the nurse called, and I asked her to leave the news on my voicemail so your dad and I could listen to it together, and she told us: *It's a girl!* And we smiled at each other, knowing the decision of your name was already made, months ago, nineteen months earlier to be exact, when I wept in your father's arms, unable to leave the bed, crushed gray with grief, and he stroked my hair, curling it behind my ear again and again and again, and it was then that he first whispered the spell which brought you to us:

Why don't we try and have a baby,
and if it's girl, we'll name her after your mom.
We'll call her Maureen.

Hand Me Downs

World's Best Brother. COOL DUDE.
Anything with dinosaurs, robots, construction trucks.
Blue with sailboats or baseball bats or soccer balls.

Maureen is too young to mind, so her sibling and I
play dress up with her, pushing her sparse brown
curls to part like a boy's might and snap photos.

*She's going to look back on these pictures
and be like whose baby is this? Who is this boy?*
I tell her sibling, laughing.

Or maybe she is a boy, and just isn't able to tell us yet,
her sibling replies, a perfect Gen Z response.
Maybe you're right, I say, gobsmacked, marveling

again at my luck to have these two kids in my life.
And so now, every month, my stepkid and I dress
Maureen in fresh boy hand-me-downs

so that whoever Maureen grows up to be,
we will be able to give her a baby photo
to match for the yearbook.

If You *Are* a Boy

your father and I will love you just the same,
of course, and will call you any name you choose.

And if you're looking for suggestions
from your mother, which all growing children do, I hear,

I want to mention that aside from Ernie Jr., and Kurt,
and Ashland Philadelphia, and Digby, I had thought

to call you Trip, to honor the two before you,
who didn't make it; and Benjamin Franklin,

because I am from Philadelphia after all; and briefly,
the male version of Maureen, which I decided was

Maurice, but wonder if that condemns you to hearing
people warble, *Some people call you a space cowboy!*

at you for the rest of your life, and so maybe scrap that one.
Names from your family tree include Jack, Stanislaus, Leon,

John, George, Henry, Daniel and Bruce (my side),
and Allen, Elmer, Riley, Wilbert, and Abraham (your dad's).

Johan, strangely, is the name of both mine and your father's
earliest American ancestor. Still, now that you exist & breathe

before us, I offer you these, that seem like they might fit:
Anwil, which means *beloved.* Didier, which means *wanted.*

Teo, which means *gift of God.* Amare, which means
Beautiful. And Rian, which is Gaellic for *little king.*

Ashland, OH

Husband, I wish I could've met the teenage you,
though surely I would have been terrified. The one time
we drove through your small hometown, you couldn't help
but point out all the places where you loved: the football field
where you shared a first kiss; the backyard where you met
your girlfriend under a boat; the fields; the backroads;
the small, beguiling homes of your high school flames.
You were a heart, wild and pumping with want. I wonder
who I could have been with you? My own teenage body,
dizzy and confused. I wanted boys so bad, I couldn't look
at them, let alone touch them. Decades later, when we are
finally able to find ourselves alone, we are like teenagers
all over again. Now, married, we sneak around, keep quiet:
two kids under our roof. We take our chances. Sometimes,
you creep into the baby's room to help her fall asleep,
pretending to sleep right next to her, holding her small hand,
and I watch with tenderness in my heart through the monitor.
I think, how lucky I am to know the older you, the father,
the husband. But then, you arrive back in the doorway,
a look in your eyes, and I realize I can have both:
the grounded father I married, and that puckish Ashland boy
who wants what he wants and will do what it takes to get it.

One Year

On the morning of her first birthday,
I read to her father parts of the birth story,
which I had remembered to write down.
And I asked him what he remembered
about that day, and he said how nice I was
to everyone, how I kept complimenting everyone
on what a great job they were doing, and how he
just wanted to say, *They all get it! Focus on you!*
and how he thought that was very *me*.

And I suppose it was, but there was something else,
some other reason I am not sure I could admit
to anyone until she was here, and here for a while.
The reason I kept complimenting everyone so much
was that I felt sorry for them. I was so sure
you wouldn't make it that I became worried for them,
how hard it'd be for them to be the ones to tell me
you were gone.

And so, I wanted them to know how much
I appreciated them in the moment, because
I knew they wouldn't believe me afterwards.
I complimented them again and again and
in this way, I accepted my fate, which wasn't
my fate. Thank God. Thank all the gods.
Thank whatever magic left in the world
that made my fate *you*.

Before We Really Knew

what was to come, but knew enough to be prepared,
we brought the baby to the grocery to stock up.
There were no cases in the city yet, and Maureen loved
riding in the grocery store carts and waving at strangers.
We thought it would be a good idea to bring her as it might
be a while before we'd be able to do it again. It was not
a good idea, we realized, as we pushed her through the doors
and into the unnerving, quiet chaos. Everyone trying to get
what they needed, darting through the aisles like fish, taking
shallow breaths. The baby cooed and waved. Everyone smiled
tightly at her, shooting me a look like, *Did you really bring a baby
to a supermarket right as a pandemic is breaking out?* I smiled,
each smile growing smaller until I turned to my husband,
who was stocking up on the only mac and cheese our oldest
eats, and before I could say a word, he said, *I know, I know,
I feel it too. We've got to get out of here.* We didn't know
what was coming, but we knew it wasn't good.

Text from My Physician Brother-in-Law about Why It is Critical to Self-Isolate, 3/13/20

Because it has the highest number of contagious
unidentified people and non-infected vulnerable people
in the general population, at 2-3 contacts away from you.
So it's very easy to be the link between someone's boss
and someone's grandma right now, even if
you only interact with young and healthy adults.

In a week you'll know who to avoid because people will say
"Oh, this person I work with got sick." And in a week,
it will literally be everyone who didn't isolate this week.

The people who go out this week and pick up the virus
will have it for ten days before they start showing signs
of sickness and they are contagious the whole time period.

The people they get sick are the ones who will die in twenty days.
And that's the wave that will overwhelm hospital capacity.

At the Beginning of a Possible Pandemic, I Dream of the Room My Mother Died In

It is more of a concept. It's not that I know I am dreaming,
but more that I know I am thinking of this room.
It's alone in space, floating. The two solid walls
to the right and left, the single window on the wall facing
me, and the wall which is glass, windows and sliding door,
is wide open. It is a jewel box before me, this place I used
to think about all the time, without warning, and now it is
coming back to me, and my therapist asks me if it makes me
weak, helpless, and I pause. Helpless, yes, I tell her.
We could not stop what was going to happen, but it is a place
of power too. I got to be there. I chose to return to that room
again and again and again as my mother negotiated coma
into death, and each time I entered, I was grateful she was
still alive, solely because I did not want to miss her death.
and I didn't.

My therapist asks me what it would take to sanctify this room:
wind, water, fire, dirt? I don't understand what she is asking.
She reframes it and it all still sounds like destruction, to destroy it.
No, no, she says, she means change it. Honor what it is to me now
as opposed to what it was then. And I tell her I will write about it,
capture it on the page, so instead of thinking about it I can read
about it when I want to visit it. And she still asks about
sanctifying it, tells me for some reason she pictures it
filled with purple flowers, and I just can't meet her there,
can't see what she wants me to do with this room I do not hate.

And that's when I realize why it may have come to me,
as a virus blossoms across the states my family lives in.
My own father, sturdy and scientific; my husband's parents,
long dead. It is hard to be away from my siblings, their children,

all trying to stay safe in an infected place, washing their hands and securing their medicine. But my love for them does not overwhelm the need my own family has for me, my children, my spouse. I can stay a thousand miles away, and fling my love like messages in a bottle through our phones. But my God, if my mother had still been alive. If she, with shaky health, had been the one who stood in the crosshairs, I would not have been able to stand it. I would have chosen my children, and my mind would have torn skin from flesh every minute with worry for her.

So this room, this altar to the death she would have wanted, that I would have chosen, if I had to choose: to be there for her. This room is a gift, I realize, this room is a gift. I fill it flowers. I gild it with gold. I praise it for what it is:
the last place my mother lived,
a place of beauty.

Turning Three During a Pandemic

I ask my daughter where she wants to go, and she says,
Inside. I want to go inside someplace. I ask her what
she would like to do, and she says, *New. Something new.*
And when I tell her why we need to stay home, why we can't
see friends, or go back to school, take that trip to see PopPop,
or Uncle Kevin, and everyone else who has been sending
her videos, hollering, *We can't wait to see you soon!!*
Only "soon" never happened, and I tell her it's because
of the virus, and she asks me to roll up the shades so
she can look at this virus. She tells me she can't see it.
And I say it's too small to see, and that's why we need
to stay safe, and this has been almost her whole life,
two birthdays with just the blood that lives in her house,
with videos of people, no different than Big Bird,
or Daniel Tiger, these friends on the other side of the screen,
and I want to tell her how they are real, she can touch them,
as soon as it is safe, and she doesn't know to ask when,
she only says, *Okay!* and runs to the dog to kiss it,
and that is what breaks my heart. How simply she lets go,
how much, how deeply, she doesn't know what she is losing,
what she has lost.

After My Vaccination

I had a feeling I would be good at nursing,
my breasts rising and rounding in my thirties.
Their tenderness was the first sign of my pregnancy,
and for weeks I would squeeze them, taking comfort
in their persistent ache. When she was born
Maureen didn't cry, she squeaked, squinting in my arms
for a bit, before moving down to my left nipple,
and it began. Now, years later, this nursing is what
is keeping her safe, the antibodies in my milk rushing
into her system, and now I want to keep her nursing,
until she can get her own shot, her own chance to survive.
Until then, I bring her back to my marriage bed,
wrap her giggling body in a heavy blanket. *Comfy, cozy*,
she tells me as she sinks her body down. I hold her,
as her father snores, as the world, with all its possibility,
waits, just a while longer, on the other side of the window.

Love in the Time of COVID

We call it the *pan-dick-inning*,
the furious love we make in quiet,
in secret, in the spaces we can find

while the kids are asleep, or on zoom.
In the early days, my husband watched me
wipe down every banana

with an antibacterial wipe, and asked
Is that really necessary? and all I could
reply is, *I don't know?*

Months later, and still the only thing
I can trust to touch is the skin
under his shirt, the thick muscle

of his thigh, his face in my hands.
When it is safe enough to send the kids
back to school, it takes us days to find

that moment again. After all, our hearts
are outside ourselves, laughing
with other kids, breathing in their air,

and all we could do was eat a nervous lunch.
check our phones, and clean all the things
that needed cleaning.

But then, love, we can see it: ourselves,
alone, and human, the house, a concert hall,
one we are happy to finally fill again with music.

On the Occasion of My Husband Going On his First Business Trip in Two Years, and Then Deciding the Very Next Day That He was Coming Home Early

They say that when something funny happens, you instinctually turn to the person you feel closest to so that you might share the laugh with them. All day, I was laughing and spinning in circles in our house, unable to find you. Although, at times, the pandemic made us feel like captives, you were never the enemy. We clung to each other, like wards of the same capricious relative, doing our chores, eating our food, and keeping all our heat hidden, but charged. When you left for the first time in years, the three of us sat on the porch and watched until we couldn't see your car anymore, and the air in the house when we stepped inside felt thinner. The next day, after dropping the kids off at school, I was home alone, truly alone, no children, no husband, the dogs snoozing at my feet. I felt like a single woman, a familiar lonesome. I tried to savor it, use it to fuel the fire of my work, but instead I got distracted by the idea of you, the flames of chest hair which lick up your stomach, and blossom on your chest. Your shoulder caps, and how they look with my fingers spread across them. The way you sit in a chair, my favorite meal, breathing in the dark. This morning, in the sterile hum of your hotel, you tell me you are coming home, you miss us too much, and you don't care for Los Angeles. You've had a good time, but have had enough. I don't talk you out of it. Instead, I walk around the house filled with the waiting, the longing. It's only been a day, but what is the point of laughing, if you aren't there to catch it?

Tambourine! Tambourine! Tambourine!

When I can steal time to write, finally, I sit quietly,
as best I can & see what rises up from me, rises out of me,
& sometimes the topics are immediate, grimy, the dirty laundry
that my poetry always tells me I don't have to wash. Other times,
the stories I've told & told & told make themselves known,
and explain that pressing them into the page seems a logical
next step. But other days, it is uncontainable. I have waited
too long, and my poetry, impatient, wants to be everything:
my longing, my lust; the entirety of New York City, so far
from my heart & already having forgotten me; Philadelphia,
my family's bloodlines unearthed this winter from its soil;
my teenager, my toddler; my husband & his beard; his shoulders;
my whole beating heart. I tell my brain to choose one thing,
make it good. My brain tells me it is all or nothing.
Tambourine! Tambourine! Tambourine! my friend Shanny
hollers when she feels like she needs to accompany her life's
miracle chaos, hoping that if she can contain it if she can make
music with it. My brain wants me to make music with it. I can't.
I tell my brain, my pages can't contain all of this at once.
Just choose one thing, I say, *please*. And I look past my desk
and through the window, where outside, the rain has made
the ground so wet, boulders keep falling out of the hills.
The thickest, heaviest rocks—what we had assumed where
the foundation of the earth we built our home on—now lay
plopped onto our lawn like spoiled fruit. I see my husband
wandering around, holding our youngest's hand, as she shrieks
with joy, at the bottom of the stones, now exposed. When I was
her age, I'd have run straight into the hem of my mother's dress,
so afraid I was of the pillbugs & spiders & centipedes & shiny
black beetles, like the living bullets of the dirt. But my daughter

is not me. She laughs, tugging her father closer, pointing,
her voice muffled by distance but not impossible to hear:
hello friend, hello friend, hello friend, see, daddy, see,
see our new friends, we didn't know they were here!
But now we can see them! Hello hello hello! Hello friend! Hello!

Oh, New York

How many poems have I written about you? Not enough, I guess.
I once wrote, *New York City has many lovers, but marries no one.*
And it's true. You are my most intimidating ex-girlfriend,
always laughing too loud, talking too fast, so much more beautiful
and worldly than any other city could ever hope to be. This past year,
I had to watch from afar as a virus tried to take you apart bit by bit,
starting with the ungrateful rich people, who left at the first hint
of discomfort, then by disease itself, which tried to crush
the greatest parts of you—not the skyscrapers, or screaming neckties
on Wall Street, but your huge, generous heart, that is already so full
and yet welcomes, and welcomes, and welcomes, and welcomes,
and presses us all together until we become a strange family.
The virus made that pressing a weapon. It made a poison of the air
in which we all once laughed, into which we all sang, and hollered,
and finally heard our own names, maybe for the first time. I shook
in Texas reading about graves being dug in parks (untrue), about nights
filled with never-ending sirens (true), about the unfathomable,
exhausting toll of grief. To fly back into you felt like a dream:
my old airport, my old neighborhood, the bridges that felt like movie sets
because they are, the friends who survived, who wrapped me up
in their warm, living arms, and let me weep onto them out of pure relief,
unbottled joy. Your streets are emptier, for now, but no less romantic.
The subway cars rattle empty, for now. The boarded-up storefronts.
Subway platforms dressed up like a holiday weekend in the middle
of the work week. The whole city sounds like a sanitized
sound machine version of itself, for now, for now. But listen:
everyone knows. Everyone. You are still *everything*. The other cities
should be jealous, New York, because I never stopped loving you,
never stopped wanting you, never stopped trying to deserve you,
showing up the moment you call, just so I can tell you to your face
that you are beautiful, even if it's just so you can roll your eyes
in response, talking about, *Oh I know, I just wanted to make sure*

that you didn't forget, before sending me away again, breathless, dumbstruck, heart-broken, heart-swollen, knocked out, filled up, radiant, and grateful, grateful, grateful.

My Little New York

White bagel. My toddler wants a *white bagel*, and I am
confused because we do not have any bagels in the house,
and also, she has never liked bagels, and yet here she is,
before I have had my morning cup of coffee, loudly insisting
she be given one. Once, I asked a bartender for the time,
and the bartender was my lover, and a poet, and he told me
the time, and I told him, *Well, I guess I better get started then,*
and I would make my way through the crowd of New Yorkers
and tourists, and they would not only part, but begin to clap,
because me moving to the stage meant the show was about
to begin, and I created this show, and I hosted this show,
and I had new poems to read later, but first I welcomed everyone
and winked at the sound guy for the great intro music, and I lived
in the same apartment I moved into after college, and I still knew
the songs on the radio, and where to get the best *artisanal* cannoli,
and which subway lines were under construction, and waiters
knew me by name, and I read books on the subway that I bought
at the Strand or Housing Works, and I loved walking the streets
just to walk them because I had the time, and the city was so loud
and beautiful and happening all the time, all the time, all the time,
all at once, and my toddler is now hollering WHITE BAGEL!
and I realize she means donut. A powdered donut. And she calls it
a white bagel because I called them "white bagels" for a reason
I cannot explain now, but which likely had to do with obscuring
the outlandish amount of donuts I was allowing her to eat, and I tell her
she can have ONE, and she agrees, and sits on the couch with it,
while our dachshunds stare lustily at her, and I steal away to make
my first cup of coffee in the part of the house my husband calls
my *Little New York* because it contains only a treadmill and
a fancy coffee machine, and as I wait for the coffee to brew,
outside, a bird I cannot see, but am certain is *not* a pigeon,
refuses to stop screaming.

Parallel

My therapist tells me that I am not
in conflict with myself.

That the old me, stripped down to metal,
grinding out my goals in an unforgiving city,

unrelenting, spare, can exist alongside
the me of now, who walks softly down

the hallways of her own house,
so as not to disturb her sleeping children,

who types faster when she hears little footsteps
so she can stop when the door flies open: *Mama!*

These are things I was sure I'd never have:
a husband, children, a house, comfort, security.

My former self doesn't know how to hold these gifts,
I tell my therapist, wants to deny them to give me fuel.

Scarcity, want, have always been where I found my power.
No, my therapist says, *just tell her.*

*Just tell her that you are happy. And then tell her
you want her to be happy too.*

On the Six-Year Anniversary of my Mother's Passing

I sometimes wonder if I will be forever frozen at the time
when you died. It is the last time I felt like myself, or, perhaps,
that is just what I tell myself. When a book ends, the author
wants you to imagine what happens next to the characters
for yourself, but mother, narrator, I don't know what I am doing.
The shaggy threads of my life which you sewed back into me.
Without you, I feel as if I am unraveling, as if I am unraveled.
Nothing adds up. I told my therapist I want to return to who I was,
changed by what I went through, but still able to fill up that space.
She told me to imagine myself as a grandmother. Imagine speaking
to my kids after they become parents. *When you are that grandmother*,
she told me, *you won't be telling your children 'Oh, I wish I had spent
that time writing more book proposals.' You will have been so happy
that you spent that time with them.* And I felt the specter
of your presence shift. Even now, when I picture the future,
I can't imagine not talking to you. You, who has been silent
for six years, except in my head. The you in my head tells me,
You are doing such a good job! But another you in my head
whispers bluntly, honestly: *You could do more.*

My Dead Ancestors
Try to Explain To Me
How I'm Missing the Point

We never wanted you to follow the rules. We never wanted you
to define success by things, by status, by money. What is it
that they say? If you want to know what God thinks of money,
look at who he's given it to. Christ, you know we've always hated
those guys. Look, you need enough for food on the table, for a roof
over your head, for surprises for the kids, and a little spare to help
the people who could use a little help. You don't need piles of it
to stare at, and you certainly don't need to rip yourself from joy,
from love, from presence, to add to that mute, heartless pile.
Jesus. When we whispered in your ear about getting out
of the neighborhood, we didn't mean nothing but *out*. Someplace
new, different, challenging. Remember how we sailed across
a black ocean, seasick and cramped in flea infested boats
just to end up in the slums of Philadelphia? Remember how happy
it made us? The children we made, adopted, raised? Remember
the boundaries we pushed, the risks we took, the lines we crossed?
You think we did that for money? We're drinking up in heaven,
honey, and when we stop laughing and dancing long enough
to look down on your dirt-bound body, we don't do it to see you
trying to make *money*. We look to see you chase the biggest joy,
the wildest dream, to laugh the loudest laugh. We want to hear you
cackling with those fat-cheeked kids of yours, surprising
your husband's ass with a horny pinch in front of mixed company,
slapping your full belly in astonishment and swearing you can't
eat one bit more, until the moment they roll in the desserts.
We want you to *live*. You'll be dead soon enough, trust us.
So stop worrying so goddamn much. Listen to your heart,
your puckish Irish gut, listen to us laughing in your ear.
Lord, we never knew what we were doing. Not once.
But we didn't do so bad, **did we? I mean, you're here,
ain't you?**

On Lowering Standards

People always act like this is a bad thing, when really,
it means you can sometimes eat cheesecake for breakfast.

Or that poems, like this one, get written. That you will make
another woman on the subway smile, thinking, *Thank God*

it's not just me as you sweatpants-n-sunglasses your way
to a happy brunch. I have been known to march in place,

desperate to clock in the final steps I needed for the day.
I've been known to submit a typo-filled application just

scratch it off the to-do list. I have told my terrified rescue dog,
This is my third time petting you today! in my long campaign

to get him to like me. I know the joys of consistency,
of keeping your word. I get it. But it's okay, friend, to let it go

sometimes. To do good enough for *right now*. Or not to.
Some days, the best choice isn't what is going to make you

hate yourself the least, it's the one that actually might make you
happy. There is a difference. Test the waters. Feel the air.

Hit the snooze. Eat the leftovers the same night as the dinner
you got it from. Make your joy the center of your world.

What I want for you is to ignore everyone else, and say,
You know, this isn't like me at all before you give yourself

the freedom to do the thing that is the absolute most
you thing ever.

She Reaches Out, Says, *I Love You*

And I say, *I love you too!*

She says, *Do you want to guess how much?*
Do you want to guess how much I love you?

I say, *How much?*

She says, *As big as this room!* swinging her arms
around into the echoing airport waiting area.

Oh yeah? I say, *Well, I love you as much*
as this airport!

Oh yeah, she says, *Well, I love you as much*
as the United States of America!

Oh yeah, I say, *Well, I love you as much*
as the Earth.

Oh yeah, she says, *Well, I love you as much*
as the galaxy!

That's so much! You love me that much? Wow!
What about you, Daddy, I ask her father.
How much do you love us?

Oh me? he says, *I love you even bigger*
than the universe, and the universe is the biggest
thing there is! It contains the Earth, and our galaxy,
and a whole bunch of other planets and a whole bunch
of other galaxies. And it's always expanding,
so it's getting even bigger all the time!
NOTHING is as big as the universe!

Well, ONE thing is bigger, I say,

No, NOTHING is bigger than the universe, he repeats. *It's always expanding, so nothing is or will ever be bigger.*

EXCEPT YOUR LOVE FOR US, I tell him.

Oh yes, he says, remembering, *except for that.*

Ownership

The way her five-year-old hands glide around my neck,
the tenderest noose, squeeze. How she wraps her legs,
her ankles around my neck, climbs up me,
planting her hard chin on the top of my head
like an American flag. It has been years since
I nursed her, but her fingers still dive into my shirt,
Or up. It's all hers. She knows it. Sometimes my mind
wanders back to the moments after my mother died,
and she laid still in that hospital bed, her gown loosened
enough to see that familiar constellation of freckles
that announced themselves every summer on her tanned
chest. *I should take a picture,* I thought, so *I can remember*
before realizing how a photograph of my dead mother
would never serve as comfort. The constellation would
be lost, like some many other things. And then my brain,
a generous remote control, switches to a different channel:
my mother, laughing on the beach, her watch fastened
on her bathing suit strap so as to not interrupt the steady,
purposeful darkening of her arms. How I would run to her,
all ages, hands wet and cold from the ocean, to fling
wrinkled fingers over the landscape of her, this body
I owned, and how she would shriek, laughing, cold droplets
exploding off of her, how she never told me to stop,
how I never did.

Present

You were not there to arrange the bridal veil
around my small round face, or admire the ring
which I inherited from your favorite aunt and
which I chose to wear as my engagement ring.
You were not there when I was surprised
to find two pink lines on the stick after sixteen
months of bust ups, nor were you there when
I lost that baby, or the next one, or spent the entirety
of the third and last pregnancy sure I would lose it,
vomiting vitamins into the toilet, crying in the dark.
You weren't there at the hospital, or the NICU.
You didn't raise the door of the garage when
we finally brought her home, your namesake,
nor did you place your strong hands on my shoulders,
kissing the part of my hair as I breast-fed her at dawn.
Except, of course, you were. Of course you were.
Mom, of course, you were. You never left my side.

Acknowledgements

Grateful thanks are given the **Hedgebrook Writers-In-Residence** program, where many of those poems were edited.

Grateful acknowledgements are made to the following journals in which some of these poems first appeared in slightly different forms:

Nailed Magazine—"17 Weeks" and "27 Weeks"
Barrelhouse Magazine—"Love in the Time of COVID"

The poem "Oh, New York" was written for and first performed at "**Working Intersections**," an evening of poetry curated by Lincoln Center's first ever poet-in-residence, Mahogany L Browne. "Working Intersections" was the debut event of the Browne's monthly virtual and in-person program for Lincoln Center entitled "We Are The Work," which served as an artistic call to recharge and unite towards justice within our communities.

IF YOU LIKE CRISTIN O'KEEFE APTOWICZ, CRISTIN O'KEEFE APTOWICZ LIKES

I Love Science
by Shanny Jean Maney

How the Body Works the Dark
by Derrick Brown

In the Pockets of Small Gods
by Anis Mojgani

No Matter the Wreckage
by Sarah Kay

The New Clean
by Jon Sands

Uncontrolled Experiments in Freedom
by Brian S. Ellis

IF YOU LIKE *AGAINST VANISHING*, CHECK OUT CRISTIN O'KEEFE APTOWICZ'S OTHER WRITE BLOODY BOOKS

Dear Future Boyfriend
In her quirky debut volume, Cristin O'Keefe Aptowicz tackles love ("Science"), heartbreak ("Lit"), and thieving suburban punks ("Ode to the Person Who Stole My Family's Lawn Gnome"), among other hilariously idiosyncratic topics.

Hot Teen Slut
In her second collection of poetry, Cristin O'Keefe Aptowicz serves up a memoir-in-verse of her first job out of college: writing and editing for porn. Aptowicz dramatizes the hopes, humor, and ambitions of a young poet's first steps into a very surreal "real world."

Working Class Represent
In her third collection of poetry, Cristin O'Keefe Aptowicz celebrates the ups and downs of being a performance poet with a day job. This book continues Aptowicz's tradition of witty, honest, and wildly original work.

Oh, Terrible Youth
In her fourth collection of poetry, Cristin O'Keefe Aptowicz uses her youth as a muse. This plump collection commiserates and celebrates all the wonder, terror, banality, and comedy that is the long journey through to adulthood.

Everything is Everything
In her fifth collection of poetry, Cristin O'Keefe Aptowicz polishes her obsessions until they gleam. Everything is Everything illuminates the dark corners of the curiosity cabinet, shining the light on everything that is utterly strange, wonderfully absurd, and 100% true.

The Year of No Mistakes
In her sixth collection of poetry, Cristin O'Keefe Aptowicz bears witness to the unraveling of a decade-long relationship. Intimate, observant, and unflinchingly honest, Aptowicz explores love, nostalgia, grief, desire, envy, and hope in poems that showcase her emblematic funny and heartbreaking style.

How To Love The Empty Air
In her seventh collection of poetry, Cristin O'Keefe Aptowicz reaches new heights. Vulnerable, beautiful, and ultimately life-affirming, Aptowicz battles the silencing power of grief after the sudden loss of her beloved mother, sharing intimate poems which transverse the landscape of her loss, and arriving on the other side still counting her blessings.

**ALL BOOKS ARE AVAILABLE ON
WRITE BLOODY PUBLISHING**
America's Independent Press

About the Author

Photo by Ernest Cline

Cristin O'Keefe Aptowicz is the author of seven previous collections of poetry—*Dear Future Boyfriend*; *Hot Teen Slut*; *Working Class Represent*; *Oh, Terrible Youth*; *Everything is Everything*; *The Year of No Mistakes*; and *How To Love the Empty Air*—which are all currently available on Write Bloody Publishing. She is also the author of two nonfiction books: *Words In Your Face: A Guided Tour Through Twenty Years of the New York City Poetry Slam* (Soft Skull Press, 2008), which Billy Collins wrote "leaves no doubt that the slam poetry scene has achieved legitimacy and taken its rightful place on the map of contemporary literature; and *Dr Mutter's Marvels: A True Tale of Intrigue and Innovation at the Dawn of Modern Medicine* (Gotham Books, 2014), which was on the *New York Times* best seller list for three months. Recent awards include a National Endowment for the Arts Fellowship in Literature, the ArtsEDGE Writer Residency at the University of Pennsylvania, the Amy Clampitt House Residency, and the Hedgebrook Residency. When not on tour, she splits her time between Austin, TX, and Philadelphia, PA.

For more information or to see upcoming tour dates,
please visit her website at:

www.aptowicz.com

www.ingramcontent.com/pod-product-compliance
Lightning Source LLC
LaVergne TN
LVHW042118020425
807577LV00015B/62